HEDGE SCHOOL

First published in 2024 by
The Dedalus Press
13 Moyclare Road
Baldoyle
Dublin D13 K1C2
Ireland

www.dedaluspress.com

Copyright © Pat Boran, 2024

ISBN 9781915629319 (paperback)
ISBN 9781915629302 (hardback)

All rights reserved.
No part of this publication may be reproduced in any form
or by any means without the prior permission
of the publisher.

The moral rights of the author have been asserted.

Dedalus Press titles are available in Ireland
from Argosy Books (www.argosybooks.ie) and in the UK
from Inpress Books (www.inpressbooks.co.uk).
Printed in Ireland by Print Dynamics.

Cover photograph, *Bees in Thyme,* by Michael Boran,
by kind permission.

Dedalus Press receives financial assistance from
The Arts Council / An Chomhairle Ealaíon.

HEDGE SCHOOL

PAT BORAN

DEDALUS PRESS

i.m. Nancy Boran (née Delany)
1923 – 2020

Contents

Hedge School / 7
As Far as Turn Back / 9
Zoom / 10
Neighbours Make a Neighbourhood / 12
Starlings / 13
Driving South / 14
The Statues of Emo Court / 15
Feather / 19
Seed / 20
Building the Ark / 21
The Window Seat / 23
Itching Powder / 24
Scythe / 26
Haggard of Sparrows / 27
Missing Children / 29
Bird Song / 32
Out of the Blue / 33
Summer in Baldoyle / 35
Ant Nest / 36
The High Window / 37
New Homes / 38
Boundary / 39
Hedgehog / 40
Seal / 41
Beggar / 42
Mirror / 44
Honey Bees / 45
Sometimes / 46
Rose / 47
Pollination / 49
Camping by the Lake / 50

Fellow Travellers / 51
Billy, Billy / 52
Advisory Note / 53
Fields under Fog / 54
Back to School / 55
Cherry Tree / 56
The Opposite of Everything / 57
The Fairy Houses of Ireland / 58
Penal Laws / 59
Persephone / 60
Greater Stitchwort / 61
Blackberry Bush / 62
Kingfisher / 63
Changing of the Guard / 64
A Goat Song / 65
A History of Pigeons / 67
Seed Bank / 72
Beyond the Hedge / 73
Slug / 74
My Mother's Books / 75
WWF / 76
The Concert / 77
A School / 78
Chevron / 79
Girl With a Pearl Earring / 80
Thatched Roof / 81
The Mistake / 83
Late September / 84

ACKNOWLEDGEMENTS & THANKS / 85

Hedge School

What's she at
   out back
that little bag
   of chirps
small beak
   hole-poking
feather-stroking
   nitpicking
stick-amassing
   her tail flashing
stitching nothing
   to nothing more
than empty air
   taking chances
with those silly dances
   playing hide and seek
on her all-alone
   and unaware
that just by being there
   in those song-sung
bone-bare
   bowed and broken branches
half her work
   is done

As Far as Turn Back

After we've walked for long enough
the conversation peters out,
and grunts, sniffs and the occasional cough
are all that punctuate the quiet.

Now and then, there's a heel-burst
slipstream of shingle; a see-saw
slate-flat rock taps and trembles
its morse code underfoot;

a crow caws, a sheep responds
from a clump of grass a field away.
But that's about the size of it.
No path agreed in advance,
we're just out walking on this lockdown day,
taking the air and, taken by it,
leaving the road for animal tracks,
heading, as my father's phrase would have it,
'as far as turn back'.

And who knew that not knowing
where that turn would turn out to be
would turn out to be
the thing we'd miss the most.

Zoom

'Sorry, it's a mess,' he says, my friend.
And he isn't wrong. Bug-eyed from being sat
too close to his screen for weeks on end,
then half a year, now long-haired and bearded
he's trapped there in his cluttered man cave,
like the back room of the local charity shop,
the floor piled high with boxes and books,
the walls obscured with crooked paintings
and mould-stain maps, the shelves
bowed down beneath the weight of toasters, pots
and ancient bric-à-brac, and to his left and right
on the litter-strewn desk so many empty bottles
that it's like the morning-after aftermath
of the far too many parties we gatecrashed
a lifetime back in a barely recognisable world,
to drink and laugh and sing our sweet heads off
before passing out, only to wake once more,
looking more or less, in fact, as he looks now —
unkempt, grey-faced, undeniably
the worse for wear. I try to be casual
but realise I stare. I want to offer him
a hug, a mug of coffee, the hair of the dog.
I want to be clear, to clear a space
in all this stacked-up debris, to draw in close
and talk with him the way we used to talk
before every word and gesture and silence
becomes untrue. Instead, as you do,
I smile a consultant's smile and wave again,
awkward as a zoo visitor briefly looking in
to some unlabelled cage, or a tourist
caught in the harsh light of midday
stepping through some oddly Gothic door

not mentioned in the Guide, to find
candles flickering, an existential trembling
of flesh and voice – and there, look, some local saint
walled in, sat patiently now for centuries, it seems,
in the small side chapel of his devotion.

Neighbours Make a Neighbourhood

i.m. Jamie 'Skipper' Moore

When Jamie died, Jamie
who I didn't really know but always
stopped to talk, in passing, never about
whatever things were happening in his life,
the treatments he was on, but about the plants
he saw me photographing in the park,
the light, about being out in good
clean air and making the best of it;

when Jamie died, his family and friends
lit up the small estate we live on
with balloons and bunting, with children's drawings,
and, in those early days of lockdown, we all turned out
to form a guard of honour along the footpaths
of the Close, the Park, the Road, the Drive,
so that at last when the hearse woke up
and we all stood there waiting, side by side
in that oddly beautiful April weather,
neighbours all but strangers to each other,

down the road and into the estate they came
on bikes, a woman and her teenage daughter,
both of them dressed as if for summer,
and as they approached and passed our corner
and the turn for Jamie's house — the girl
just then catching up with her mother —
I heard the mother's half-whisper of delight:
'Oh look,' she said, taking in the crowd
of smiling faces all around them. 'It must be a wedding.'

Starlings

Like the warm-up notes
of the orchestra,
the frills and thrills,
the two-step stop
and return
to start again,
the creak and peep
and pirp and paaawp,
the ruffle of papers
the cough, the tap-tap
almost-ready second-last
last-second warning,
the first few starlings
then the entire performance,
wrapped in its own
round and sound of applause,
comes spilling in.

Driving South

Driving south in the sunshine,
the music loud, the flag of wind
flapping wildly in the rolled-down windows;
to either side, islanded in green,
glimpses of abandoned farmhouses
seen... seen... unseen... Above
in the higher hills, a stand
of slowly revolving turbines
keeping imaginary time
and, now, as if from nowhere
the drumming sweet tattoo
of a swarm of bikers, first
in the rear-view mirror then
passing two abreast beside us,
all leather and chrome, all studs
and death's head insignias,
no signals, no contact, no smiles,
as if they were dreaming
the world they are facing
together alone, outriders
of our weekend retreat into nature,
tears, as they go storming past us,
streaming from their eyes.

The Statues of Emo Court

Children adore them, adults seem blind,
the wildlife are all devotees:
the squirrels and beetles, the butterflies,
the crows that confer in the trees …

Spiders spinning webs in their limbs,
moss on their shoulders and knees,
as if they were dreaming, the statues of Emo
are out here to practise Tai Chi.

Days and nights are like tides on the move;
the light fades, then inky black
darkness advances, our bleakest thoughts –
faces trapped behind glass.

Now the statues on their plinths of stone
are like pieces left behind
when some strange game of chess is abandoned —
games, the last things on *our* minds …

Here, there, alone, together,
wounded they convalesce,
whole worlds reduced to these small circles.
They remind us of ourselves.

Weeks turn to months, and overhead
the bright calligraphy
of cloud on sky is swept aside
until all the mind's eye can see

is the soft machine of the lake starting up
and, slowly emerging from fog,
the tree line, the chimneys, the Big House itself,
and these figures I've long come to love:

the jogger facing her long road alone,
the young mother on the school run,
the postman bringing news of the world,
of things done, and so much undone.

This morning there's sunshine and promise,
but even when frost grips these fields
the battered statues of Emo Court
are out here to practise Tai Chi.

One has an elbow that's bare to the bone,
others are fresh amputees,
yet nothing, not weather, not worries, not woes
prevents them from practising Tai Chi.

Through hardships nigh unimaginable,
through insult and injury
the scattered statues of Emo Court
all the while practise Tai Chi.

⁀)

I CAME HERE FIRST with my mother,
that seems a lifetime ago,
then slowly our roles were exchanged as we strolled.
When I looked she'd already grown old.

But the way she would stroke the cheeks of my boys,
both long since taller than me
in the blink of an eye, was a gesture distinct
as a movement out of Tai Chi.

And back in the days of the Big House itself,
the kitchens all bustle and steam,
the gardens rich with pheasant and fowl,
the lake full of rudd, perch and bream,

imagine the lady's maid sat up in bed,
the pantry girl roused from her sleep
slipping outside under cover of nightfall
to meet the young men of their dreams;

the treasures of empire heavy on shelves,
the brasses and trophies a-gleam,
while they danced in their night-shifts, or wished that they might,
like the statues that practise Tai Chi.

The Jesuits too in their time came and went,
the leaves shed by time's tree,
the statues consigned to the depths, so it's said,
holding their breath for years.

I've watched them since I can remember,
their poise, their fragility,
while we pass by in a relative blur
slaves to industry.

Some nights in a small frame of moonlight,
some days under inches of snow,
with nothing much other to do with their time,
and nowhere else to go,

spiders spinning webs in their limbs,
moss on their shoulders and knees,
as if dreaming, the statues of Emo,
patiently practise Tai Chi.

AND WHO CAN SAY what's in the future,
where the path up ahead might yet lead.
But the light will return to admire the resolve
of these statues that practise Tai Chi.

Text of a poetry film made in Emo Court, Co. Laois, Ireland

Feather

In the attic's closed-in sky —
a lone feather. Yesterday, nothing;
today this trace, this record
of flight or flight undone, the gap
between brick and beam
the barest grin
and scarcely wide enough to admit
an envelope of air. Outside
the creaking, groaning craft
that is this home, this life,
that strains on rolling waves,
the distant call of birds
on the wing, of a world
carrying on (if only
one breath at a time)
through relentless wind.
But up here, where the ladder's hands
are raised in surrender,
where yellowed insulation wool
is the ridge of cloud
that heralds the coming storm,
neither single word nor missive
but, clear as day,
(or night when I pull this string
and the light goes out)
some form of ending,
some leave-taking:
a cryptic signing-off,
a quill set down.

Seed

The bus station, Vilnius, late spring,
and downstairs, in the warren of shops and booths —
among the soft drinks and cigarette machines,
the phone repairs and half-price trolley bags —
is a small glass-windowed kiosk selling seeds.

Seeds and only seeds (who would have guessed)
in coloured paper packets on wire frames —
carrot, onion, lettuce, rocket, chive
and pomegranate, could it be? — a bright array
of plants and flowers I struggle to recognise.

The clock is ticking. My bus is about to leave.
And still I can't convince myself to go
but stand here watching the nothing happening:
the young assistant, sat there all alone,
lost in the troubled waters of her screen,

suddenly now a figure out of myth,
charged with keeping calm while all the world
is in constant random motion here about us,
her mind attuned to patterns overlooked,
to the longer cycles of the greater journey,

while headlong towards departure gates we push
through a leaf-storm of discarded ticket stubs.

for Greta Thunberg

Building the Ark

As a boy every time it rained for long enough
I used to wonder if the time had come
to take up tools and venture out
into my father's shed
to build the ark.

How real, how heartfelt
something in that Bible story was,
old Noah, in terror of destruction,
for days and nights on end
down on his knees, the waters
rising in all directions;

and those innocent beasts,
hoping they might yet become his friends,
lining up obediently in pairs,
as if that might make all the difference,
as if that might help them stand out from the rest.

Something in it struck a chord in me.
I'd gathered frogspawn from a local pool
to watch it hatch, a bowl of punctuation,
but which of all those wriggling glyphs
was I supposed to choose?

I'd stood in awe of older lads
who came, invariably in twos,
long after dark to our back yard,
armed with only flashlights and hessian sacks,
scaling the rusted downpipes without a thought
to lamp the hapless pigeons in their roosts.
In the faint light weeping from their bulbs,
how did they choose which to take and breed,
and which to lose?

Back then I couldn't walk the full length of the street
but stopped to greet each lonesome dog
that stood by patiently to guard the public space.
I loved the scut, the whelp, the runt
at least as much as any so-called purebred pup.
If the choice were mine, I'd populate my ark
from the local pound: with the rescue mutts,
then the one-legged gull from our neighbour's roof,
or the half-blind mule, rough as an unstuffed couch,
that decades back rested its snout
in my palm for a moment —
and has yet to lift it out.

And how did Noah ever resolve
the sleeping arrangements of lions and lambs,
of piranhas, sharks and whales,
or, standing on deck as the packed ark
at last rose off its blocks to slip out over the waves,
establish the ground rules
for woodpeckers, woodlice, woodworm?

I've loved the story for a lifetime now,
but it seems this best-known version's
got it wrong. It's not that Noah
saves the animals but that the animals,
as ever, save the man:

in times of overwhelming fear,
in times of sleeplessness and strife,
the cause that lifts the eye, the mind,
the troubled heart, the point of focus
in the flooded landscape of our lives.

*Text of a poetry film made at the Tree of Life,
St. Anne's Park, Raheny, Dublin*

The Window Seat

Our old computer motherboard, covered in dust,
looks like a city block in the holocaust

of civil war, without tanks or troops,
the buildings abandoned, the schools and shops

ghosts of themselves. Just last night,
baking bread, I saw the same pale light

in a landscape of flour, and struggled to sleep
as small mounds of dough became bodies under sheets.

I've tried classic books, but the words refuse
to make sense of the endless senseless news.

So, these mornings, this window seat
is where I find myself, nursing hot tea

and staring into space. Helpless at first
against doubt, the dark, the hurt,

I offer a blank canvas to the blaze
of streaming photons that flood these troubling days,

then watch till something moves in the dust and smoke,
and reach for that. In trust. In gratitude. In hope.

for the 10th anniversary of Laois Arthouse

Itching Powder

Rose hips, they must have been.
It's already fifty years or more,
yet I've never thought about it since

in all that time, until this moment:
the game we played, in the sloping field
beside the Brothers primary school

where those small bright red capsules
would be picked off that mysterious plant
that grew through the perimeter hedge,

and, after a chase, a wild scramble
in the grass, a pinch of the 'powder' within
would be dropped whole or drip-fed down the back

of an opponent's shirt, or of your own
(in the frenzy of writhing forms),
before you'd kick and shove to disengage,

scrambling apart like separated dogs,
and laughing hysterically now
to see in your opponent's eyes

the pain sent coursing through your veins,
the burn and sting of it, the panic
as if some living, some vicious thing

were trapped against your flesh, the sight
of boys tearing off their clothes as they ran
hilarious and terrifying all at once.

So much, then, for my hedge school thesis.
Unless what we learned there, as we learn
from hedges everywhere, was the truth about limits:

that suffering together is not the same
as suffering alone, that screaming and falling
and later admiring the scratch marks on our backs

in the bathroom mirror, bad as it was,
was still far better than being called out
one at a time in a silence expanding like a mist

across the surface of dark lake water, then coming back,
head down, and not one word of explanation,
to sit and stare ahead at the clouded blackboard

for hours on end, until the day was over,
until the living things of earth might rise and close
around you like a wall, like curtains drawn,

behind which only laughter, only whispers.

Scythe

I saw the scythe, the grim reaper's
question mark, that great, steel, glinting,
biting blade, that number seven, biblical
in its horror, edge through the long grass,
folding life into death, the seed heads collapsing,
the seeds released and broken and spread
in a cloud, in a fog, in a veiling of dust,
folding and overlaying and overlapping, layer
upon layer, as the long bright asking of it slipped
between serried ranks of grass and chambers of air
opened and hollowed where rabbits ran, where foxes —
who knew? — slipped in and out of civilization, in
and out of view, from one world into the next,
where the scythe blade now simply swept
all in its path, all with a sound
like a summoning up of silence,
the summer's summary, but soft as breath.

Haggard of Sparrows

Not a 'host', as one dictionary suggests,
or a 'flight', or a 'flock', or a 'choir'
or any of the rest that might come to mind
when you first hear them
fired up and full of life,
the racket of birds near the rear of the house
as evening came on, for my father
was ever a 'haggard' of sparrows,
the dialect word, more common then,
for a closed space, the unroofed storage
between house and wider world.

And he used it liberally
for all loud commotions, from public celebrations
to the excited conversations
of a group of passing schoolgirls ...

Small surprise then to discover
along the forking paths of a few old journals
that my father's 'haggard' (from the Old Norse
meaning hay-yard) is often confused
with the haggard that means half-starved
and gaunt-looking, or the haggard
that refers to a wild female hawk
in her adult plumage, or to a hag or witch,
from *hag,* the Old High German word
meaning hedge.

Once more back to hedge, that neighbour
of difference, of otherness, that place
where town meets country, here
meets elsewhere, where outside peers in
in the dead of night, and into or over which
by day the sparrows of the scene arrive

in dribs and drabs, then in dabs then dabbles then droves,
excitement's ambassadors, their heads
perpetually in a spin.

   for Mary Bennett

Missing Children

'Can I interest you,' the voice says, 'in missing children?'
There's a middle-aged, heavy-set black woman
out of nowhere, standing by my side.
She speaks softly, avoids eye contact.
Have I heard her right? To be honest
I'm not entirely present in the moment.
Morning? Evening? I hardly know what time
of day it is. For a start I'm probably jet-lagged,
and, after all, amazed to be at last
on the film set of the mind that is New York.
It's the late '90s, the first few hours
of my first-ever trip to *these United States,*
and I've just stepped out of Grand Central Station
to take it all in, making this, odd as it seems,
my first unscripted interaction.

The yellow taxi cabs pass by in a rage.
A kid on a skateboard risks his life for nothing.
In an alley somewhere, steam is surely leaking
from the back grill of some noodle place, Chinese or Korean.
God knows how I imagined it would be
up close, once my eyes descended from the heights.
But for sure not this. 'Can I interest you …'
She seems about to start again, then stops.
Fatigue or a kind of practised nonchalance
has lent a distance to her voice, a softness
that could be hurt, an otherness to the way
she hovers here beside me and, somehow, herself.
And as she stalls in her own lost moment,
or flicks the index cards of possible conclusions
to a wasted day, at last my eyes drift down to settle
on the blue folder spread open on her forearm,

a sheaf of plastic sleeves in each of which
(she flips — half-bored? half in a dream?) there is
a page of photographs, a neatly laid-out grid —
three by four, or it might be four by six —
like football trading cards back in my school days,

but these are all of children's faces:
white, black, Latino, Asian,
in pigtails and braces, in button-down shirts and bows,
in gold- and steel- and horn-rimmed glasses,
faces looking out from childhood bedrooms,
from school assemblies, cropped from family portraits
taken at Christmas or New Year's maybe
or the mystery that is, for me, Thanksgiving.
The images badly copied in the days
before cheap scanners and Apple laser printers,
these are the young, the bright, the legion
missing children of America.

Had I awoken, had something then been able to clear
the fog in my brain, I might have spoken
some simple words of human compassion,
beyond the meaningless grunts and awkward shrugs
I hear and see from others passing to left and right —
the palm held up, the head dropped down
between the shoulders, the quickened pace ...
But *Can she interest me* ... What does it mean?
Whatever she might want of me, an alien
in that place, a newly touched-down time traveller,
whatever I might have replied, all chance
of clarity is gone. Without another word from her,
I see her moving off along the footpath *(the sidewalk)*
to join the rest of her fellow interrogators,
all female, all black, and all of an age,
all themselves now looking strangely lost

as they wait for someone, maybe, to pick them up
and spirit *them* away,

                        while I'm left there
to stand, to stall, to stare,
the bystander who fails to react until too late,

until a small but troubling encounter begins to ring
like a low bell somewhere, ghost or echo
of the story of a teenage girl back home
in another world, picked up on the road
only miles from home and, somehow,
never — not ever — seen again; then the rumours,
then the whispers, then the hum of silence
that swells to take her place.

And now I'm moving off myself as well,
through temple doors, it starts to feel like,
to follow in this massive vaulted space
the signs saying *Subway,* though more like *Underground*
no place before or since has ever felt: the huge dead weight
of travel in my bones — the dank air
rising like a face to meet my face,
the steel-toothed escalator slowly grinding down.

Bird Song

Small bird singing in a tree.
Who's it singing for but me?

So what if it's a warning call
to rival birds beyond the wall,

the singing has a second thread
that finds the heart before the head.

And what it's saying, I suppose,
is *Stop, look — blue sky, red rose.*

*These bright things do not last for long,
God knows.*

Out of the Blue

i.m. Kevin Page

Out of the blue, out of a night
as blue and quiet as this,
some charge in the air, the sea and sky as one,

first the tips of their sails, their towering masts,
then the rippling progress of their dark and heavy oars
through shallow water;

out of myth and into history
they came, with each step the lace of tide
torn and remade, the damp sand
crunching underfoot, gulls screeching,
the Brent geese taking to the wing to spread the news,
a perfect arrow loosed into the air …

Often I pause here to imagine them,
the ones who first made landfall on this coast,
the mist lifting, threads of smoke over scattered settlements,
glimpses of lives so like the ones they'd left.

And who knows for sure what brought them,
what forced them out of home and over the waves,
the dark- and the fair-haired, the fierce
and the frightened. Who knows what they felt
when ours were the mystical islands
rising into view?

But if we too were lost, uprooted,
maddened by failure of crops,
by murder and malice and threat, were we
to be cast out onto the tide by hunger
and need, no matter our creed
we too might think of this coastline —
these sandbars and mudflats, each cliff face
and inlet and cove — as the gods' own reward.

And heartsore, maybe, we'd step ashore here
to start our lives over, only to hear,
in the still of the night, under blanketing starlight,
the restless turning of oars.

Summer in Baldoyle

Two centuries back, Samuel Lewis
in his *Topographical Dictionary of Ireland*
recorded 12 children attending a hedge school
in Baldoyle. Maybe in the ruins at Grange
or nearer to the holy well of Donaghmede,
or somewhere in the then wild lands of Mayne.
Now that I try to see them in my mind's eye,
in truth I spy them everywhere: in every clutch and clique,
every *clot,* as we used to call it back home in Portlaoise
when we met up to hang around and watch
the world go by — outside the Applegreen,
beside the Racecourse chip shop, along the low wall
of St Laurence's Church: the hedge schools
are in session. Even now, information is being swapped
and news passed on. *There is not a hedge, my Liege,
in the entire Barony of Coolock, or in all the land —
no stand of trees or reeds or weeds without
its heedless, nay rebellious summer song.*

Ant Nest

The ants beneath the flagstones are head-down
at whatever it is ants do, though it involves, for sure,
a great deal of toing and froing, of slipping out
and quickly back in out of view, activity
markedly different than when, late evenings mostly,
clear of sunlight and with the garden to themselves,
they emerge from deep-slit trenches and
fan out right and left, as though one creature
rousing itself from sleep. And then they seep
and flow and crawl into and over everything,
a living blob, an upwards leak
of otherness, a spurt of inky punctuation.
And here and there, now and then, first one
then ten, then twenty, thirty, sporting
brand-new silver see-through fold-out wings,
fluttering and flapping as they go, limp-walk
in clumsy ever-smaller circles, as if
security must be surrendered now for flight's
slim possibility, their haste
and panic in evidence long before I, reluctantly,
given the role of home-owner and death's
chief engineer in flip-flops, vest and shorts,
rain down upon them and their subterranean realm
one and then a second pot of boiling water,
around my feet a scene of stark and biblical slaughter,
while all the while the dog, kept locked inside,
as I am counting ants and slits and steps and pots,
pushes his nose against the back door glass
and cries — *cries* — cries like a poet confusing
his own pain for mourning the greater loss.

The High Window

My father locked his keys
into the four-storey
old mill building
he used as a joinery store,
so it was up to me,
aged, I'm guessing, fourteen,
and straight out of school,
to start slow-climbing
the ladder he'd borrowed
from the house next door,
higher than its roof,
higher than the trees
that ringed and rounded
and set it back from the road,
my two knees knocking,
the ladder, spineless as rope,
bending and rocking,
bile in my throat,
until I reached the gaping hole
and clambered in, the leaves
in rolling waves below me,
my clothes stuck to my skin,
the huge dark craft of the place
lurching and leaning,
the river that had ceased
to flow through it
a hundred years before
now roaring in my ears.

for David Cooke

New Homes

New homes are being built from scratch
in days or hours, in garden hedgerows,
in rotten fencing, under the eaves
or in a stack of oil-black bamboo rods
left out since last year in all weathers.
In Turkey, in Syria, people like us
are on their knees in the perishing cold,
hammering, digging, holding their breaths,
listening for the signs of movement
in the rubble that used to be their lives.
I can scarcely watch. And here,
mere feet from my garden bench,
a wave, a blur, a shoal of small dark forms
comes winging in, whirring, tumbling
through the air, life's effervescence,
soon to build a whole new glorious city
from the debris of the old. Make no mistake:
the world is cruel and beautiful in equal part.
So what to do? I write and give up writing,
and write again and again give up —
while to each new horror, each growing threat,
the birds say *no, not now, not like this, not yet.*

Boundary

Carnage of leaves and mangled branches,
every plant of that first hedge we planted
torn up overnight, destroyed
and scattered across the garden and the road.

Decades on, it bothers me yet.
Was it something we did, something we said?
Or some undirected youthful energy
that, like troubled weather, clears eventually?

Forewarned, for the next attempt
stronger plants were chosen, planted closer
and duly took. And soon the hedge
was thriving, the old wound grown over.

So, likely, I am the last one left
still dwelling on this, still trying to make sense
of a senseless act, the done-and-dusted story
neither history nor memoir, but the itch of poetry.

Hedgehog

When the hedgehog came
over the concrete slabs,
the loose gravel and various sundry obstacles
to my friend's back door,
it was, we reckoned, to take
a sip from the milk left out
for the two house cats the evening before.

But we were all so drunk and stoned
and hungover from lack of sleep
that we just sat there in the darkness and watched
from inside the sliding door

until it dawned, on the hedgehog first,
then gradually on the rest of us,
that daylight was slowly advancing
towards the house and soon
it would be time to be getting on —

though of course now we all had to sit and wait
for the slowest mover of our slow-moving troop
to finish up his business, to lap up
with a tongue like a small pink postage stamp,
what was, it turns out, no better for him
than what we'd spent the night until then
consuming. Such
are the benefits of hindsight,
when it eventually comes.

Seal

Day after day
to the same grey
landlocked bank of stones
I've come
setting time aside
to watch the looping
lowered-shoulder turn
of wave after wave,

and hoping,
before the light might fade,
to catch a glimpse:
the glint of silver opening,
the shining skinhead
whiskered grin,
the twin dark stars
of the bright-eyed visitor
that bobs and stitches,
pitches and holds his own
out there alone
through the now
wind-ruffled,
now stretched taut
steel sheet of water.

All to no avail.

Days later,
and what have I got to show?
A head cold, a sore backside,
and, on my own old skin,
only this fleeting
if somewhat otherworldly glow.

Beggar

He tells me he is trying to get to Mayo,
on the far side of the country, this scar-faced,
drink-stinking, bloodshot-eyed beggar
who approaches the table with an outstretched hand.
Patrons stiffen, check or straighten bags,
scan the footpath for a waiter or a bouncer.
He tries to look me in the eye but struggles to focus.
He is my age, maybe younger, but I feel
like a boy against his lifetime
of pain and graft. I chance a smile
and when he scowls back in confusion
like an angry dog that fails to conjure fear,
without thinking, lightly, I touch him on the arm,
and when he doesn't shake me off, just stares,
my hand settles to his shoulder (I cannot
help myself.) Now we lean in
close together, like strangers
meeting in a clearing in a jungle,
Are you sleeping rough? I ask,
with the privilege of one who is not.
He nods, wordlessly. *That's a tough gig.*
His boxer's nose might be metallic
in its leathery sunburned pouch of skin,
like – and now I see it, see him –
the bog man in the National Museum
around the corner, his eyes
trapped behind the moment's cabinet glass.
I give him a note and coins I see he scarcely
remembers asking for. He grips them
in a giant, bare-knuckled fist and,
not a word of thanks, no salutation

of one brother to another, not so much
as a grunt, and he is moving, sloping off,
a man who has been to the edge of the known
and, in a clearing, met and was touched by a ghost.

Mirror

You look in the mirror and see someone —
a relative, it might be, an old school friend,
some half-familiar — pretending to be you:

your face, but thinner; your eyes,
but darker, tired; your hair, but flat
and lifeless. You twist and turn,

Shift and gurn. You frown and squint,
a stranger in a pub at closing time.
You bare your teeth like some wild creature

imprisoned behind glass. You lean in close
until your breath appears, the test
of life they hold above the corpse.

And then you tell yourself that's quite enough
of this indulgence. When were you ever
happy with the servant who showed up

when you called out at night or rang the bell
then stood there waiting in the empty entrance hall,
checking the time, fixing your collar, full of yourself.

Honey Bees

It's said that honey bees
were introduced to Ireland
barely a mile from here

when St Modomnoc
sailed from Anglesey
into Kilbarrack,

a hive of honey bees
unnoticed
clinging to his mast.

I imagine him when he landed,
drawing his small craft
up and through the tide

into the grip of sand
and stones (a kiss
much like a lover's kiss),

and the wings of all those honeybees
beating wildly about his head
(at 230 times per second),

and all the flowers of Berach's Church,
and of all the sainted lands of Ireland,
falling in love with him then,

powerless before him,
spreading their petals
to this new, ecstatic song.

Sometimes

for MK

When music is playing, when old fingers are held
to a young cheek, when food is set down
on the cleared and just-dressed table
(it takes but a flower or two, a jug
of water, a basket of fresh-cut bread) there is
so much to talk about, to be grateful for.
Other truths must wait for other occasions.

But then, in a moment, the time comes round,
and it is now, and death has not quite entered
but stands in the doorway of the room,
bold, uninvited, refusing to retreat,

and the price of this life you love so much
is that some small creature suffering in the cold,
some beautiful wild energy, its leg trapped
between rocks, broken beyond repair,
or some true and faithful companion
struck down somewhere by a passing car
has come to the end of her journey,

and there is no one now on earth but you
to don the heavy cloak of responsibility,
to venture out beyond the soft warm glow
of the civilised world, beyond the harsh yard-lights
or the edge of tarmac into the tall, dry grass
by the side of the road, advancing
with a steady pace and clenched fists
where, all your life until this very moment,
an open hand was your sole expression of love.

Rose

I cut it back hard, Eamon,
not as well or, God knows,
as often as I should, as you'd expect
of a man of my age. But haste
is long since part of who I am
by now, the headlong dash
that sees peripheral things get done
as if by accident. And, I suppose,
nothing's more peripheral than a hedge.

So when the time comes, I gird myself —
then up and at it. Leaves and dustmotes
everywhere. A whirlwind
of that'll-do-it, good-enough-for-now
precision.

But no matter how
it goes, I always slow
almost to a stop for that one rose
here before our circus troupe
showed up, before the hedge
and the world it's helped sketch in
defined us yet. I always think
I'll find some new solution
to what to do with it, to its sticking out
of the flat (OK relatively flat)
stand of green, though roses
are another world for me. Each time
I swear I'll do it right, trim it
gently now or, better, hard and close,
like a real, finally a grown-up gardener,
but still with care, because

something there, something
in this lifeforce we can only see
in what shows up above the surface,
is bigger, Eamon, bigger than we know.

for Eamon Earley

Pollination

Of the fifty or sixty, at most one hundred bees
I've seen so far this spring and early summer
in our small back garden, who is to say
which one was responsible

for the pollination of our Elstar apple tree,
the one that stands on its own off to one side
of our modest space, while its twin partners
survive in a pair of smaller matching tubs
closer together;

and who is to say which erratic,
which unpredictable thread of string-time,
which interstellar journey between one turning planet
and the next (for time is distance, time
is space), between one photon and the next,
between alpha and omega, home
and destination, between the latest
unbearable loss and the far too early
settling for the crumbs of hope,

who now is to say
not just which bee it was, but which
minute body hair, which pollen basket and on which leg
or part of which leg — trochanter, femur,
tibia, basitarsus, pretarsus — or, if a wing,
which wing (fore- or hind-, left or right?)

so precisely manoeuvred her into place,
and, specifically, against all odds,
which wing beat was it that rescued us this year —
I can't say why but I need your answer, Lord —
and on the downward, was it, or the upward stroke?

Camping by the Lake

Years back, at the end of a path
into darkness, I pitched a tent
of dew and breath and lit a fire
that sent stars shooting up
into the Heavens.

The next morning I awoke
beside a glittering lake,
the young birch trees
tentative as deer
gathered along the shoreline
to sip from their reflections.

I didn't want to leave. In truth,
a part of me is out there
yet. But those trees
have grown and spread
and aged by now. So who can say
precisely where I slept,
or when.

Only that, on perfect mornings
such as this, that fly-plucked surface
slowly wakes to listen
for the splash of roach or rudd or perch,
or to record, in trembling ripples
spreading ever outwards,
the day's first footsteps
however far I've strayed.

i.m. Anne Merriman

Fellow Travellers

The local Traveller camp by the side of the road
is a patch of resistance, history
reduced to a circle of wagons, a tangle
of children and pets, and all the indifferent world
flowing endlessly by. But there was that time,
thirty years back, more, when busking out west
I hitched a lift in a grimy HiAce van,
climbing in from the cold only to clamber up
and over a shifting field of deep-pile rugs
and fitted sheets. Inside, a trio
of teenage girls and an older figure I took
to be their aunt, cross-legged in the gloomy,
oil-smelling dark, and all of them highly amused
by my sudden appearance out of thin air —
amused and, as it happened, unexpectedly shy.
We smiled at each other at first, scarcely speaking
beyond mumbled *howayas* and names, until, outside,
blurred by the curtain of rain and our gathering speed,
the settled and unsettled worlds went hurtling by.

Billy, Billy

The buzz, the flit, the little skip or half-a-skip
as he came to a stop; the fizz, the flicker
of something bigger than life — the pure delight
in chance encounter: *Howaya, howaya* ... followed
by a rushed account: where he was going, where
he'd been, the hum and purr of his engine heart
never idling; that glint in his eye, the dance
of his fingers, the blinking, visible thinking,
that always open grace; and the smile on his face
even as some invisible line pulled taut
and, quick as he'd come into sight, with a flick
of his fringe, head down for a marathon race
to the top of the street, or beyond, he was off and away,
blessing the world with small prayers, with a wave,
the path of his progress around and around and around,
a map of the heart of a town time can not erase.

i.m. Billy Dargan

Advisory Note

On the drive out to your burial on the Heath,
just before the hospital, Tom, I turned,
without thinking, right onto the Block Road,
then realised I was about to, yet again,
pass the house and the family filling station
where you and Nancy lived for all those years;

and as I drove past it, and the twin graveyards
right next door (both bypassed for the sun-
flooded beauty of An Fraoch Mór),
I glanced down out of simple habit

at Google Maps, still open on my phone,
where the live update read 'Maxol, Bracken's'
followed by 'not too busy' — you'd have laughed, I'm sure —
a less than illuminating advisory note.
As if the heart ever worked like that.

i.m. Tom Bracken

Fields under Fog

What do fields do? They take the rain
and soak it in. They take their time,
wave small flags for insects, bees and birds.
They do green best, but now and then
erupt in white and yellow, purple, poppy red …

They hide wild creatures, embrace a town.
They feed and nurture, get mowed down
then grow back up again.

They're like our children, always there
until they're not — until, dressed for winter,
we're left gasping, leaning on a rusted gate,

and now they're nowhere.

i.m. J.D.

Back to School

A teacher all your adult life,
each year you met the first-day kids
nervous in the classroom doorway —
their half-empty bags, their hand-me-down skirts,
jumpers and freshly ironed shirts
strange and stiff on narrow shoulders.
Now, years on, you meet them still,
transformed, reimagined, everywhere:
in the coffee shop, the checkout queue,
on the corner of the street up town,
walking the dog, pushing a pram,
waiting for the traffic lights to change.

And, late one evening, heading home,
at a Garda roadblock where, minutes before,
a fatal accident has taken place
(the flashing blue light lending the scene
a slow-motion, underwater pace),
you roll your window down to see,
in the face that now replaces your own
puzzled expression, the briefest of hints
of doubt, is it, of hesitation,
and you want to say, but can't any more —
such are the rules of the grown-up world —
'It's OK, take your time, you're doing great.'

Cherry Tree

Things we never planted take their time,
and then, when we look elsewhere, up they come:
montbretia, the so-called back-to-school plant,
mint and blackberry, daisy and dandelion ...

Even the old cherry tree I had to cut down
when we first moved here, to reclaim the space
it had grown too big for, though I dug
and cut, and cut and hacked, in truth at roots
that might have been the roots of something else,
by the time the builders came and did the job
properly, you said, with their professional machines,
ready to pour the concrete for the foundations,
there was our friend cherry, back up again,

a bonsai version of itself this time;
but, weirdly, in the space above its crown
(if crown it might be called, at that small size)
all I could see was the tree no longer there,
its pink-white blossoms drifting on the air
as they still do in our living room come springtime.

The Opposite of Everything

Willows trailing in the reflection
of trailing willows
which are really praising willows —
that is willows with their arms upraised.

The opposite of everything that's true
is true. The sun rises. We spend
but a short time on this earth, my love.
The sea is blue.

The Fairy Houses of Ireland

Those little fairy houses that started to appear
on one then fifty trees in the local park

in the early days of lockdown — made or maybe bought
by loving parents, tacked on to the bark, no doubt

to the irritation of park keepers, bird-watchers
and tree-lovers — in the way of such things

are run-down now, ghostly and haunted, their paint
flaking, their windows behind cataracts of dust.

It isn't even winter yet but already it seems
the trees are in mourning for what's been lost —

the dream of safe shelter for our own,
of refuge for those with nowhere else to turn.

So follow the news, but now and then go down
to the park, and look at them there,

those faded, fractured fairy houses — in a real sense,
the art of war. Each chill and frost,

each passing shower of rain or hail
reduces them. Each morning finds them

more true, more telling, more raw.

Penal Laws

On the morning news, stories of the Taliban
closing schools, depriving girls
of education … It's hard not to think

of our own dark days, the Penal Laws
that drove the 'hedge schools' underground:
across the land in sheds and barns, under cover

of bush and bramble, children
of the so-called 'non-conforming faiths'
gathering in secret to learn by rote,

to rehearse their tables, to recite their verses
in which freedom's many proliferating names
were, if not more potent, then surely all the sweeter

for being shared, close in, close up,
between lip and ear, all the harder to erase
for being written in breath, on air.

Persephone

*for the parents of the women still missing
in Ireland's 'vanishing triangle'*

When Persephone was taken and carried off
to the underworld, Demeter her mother
was beside herself with grief. Life
meant nothing now without her daughter. The world
became an alien, hostile place. Except that the gods
drugged her to sleep, she might have perished
from her anguish.

It's summer now, though grey skies
persist. Every day we take a walk
to stay sane, to be out and, being out,
come back again to where we find ourselves
in a new beginning.
                              But forget the myth.
Imagine, if for all the time we've been together,
for all these light-blurred months and years,
imagine she had never once returned
with light in her eyes, with spring in her gift.
Imagine we had waited and gone on waiting,
had searched and never ceased to search
except when we had passed out from exhaustion.
Imagine heartache on such a scale, all the seasons
reduced to one, a darkness that went on forever …
That is what it means to love Persephone.

Greater Stitchwort

Blackthorn and white-, hornbeam and elm,
a staff or two of silver birch,
higher up the longer-fingered
chestnut leaves, the somehow aquatic
curve of the leaf of the oak,
the giant handprints-on-sky
that is the sycamore,

and down here below,

where at first it looks like only darkness,
like the nothingness on which so much depends,
this great effusion, a whole new vault
of life — the worts and the weeds, the tangled
and angled, the inclined and entwined,
the puzzle and jumble of the whole, close-up
mess of life in all its wild confusion,

and here, and there again,
the clear expression, nay
the mildest of mild protrusions —
a flower so pale, so perfect,
so fragile and uncertain
it can only be the future.

Blackberry Bush

The common blackberry bush
grows low and dense by the path,

but hesitates, or is cut back hard,
close to the edge.

Instead, it puts out two,
no, a tiny cluster of flowers —

look sisters, brothers, friends —
to make of this latest setback

a celebration.

for Seamus Hosey

Kingfisher

As far as one might imagine
from a human king, sat on a throne
at a self-imposed distance from the action,
the kingfisher finds a rock, a reed, a twig,
and perches on it as if he were its flower,

the blue and orange plumage
less livery than passage of light,
the tiny eyes tuned in to every flash and flicker,
every stitch and glitch that shudders
on the surface of the water.

And then, no holding back, no more
remaining other any longer —
the mesh of the moment opened,
in he goes, and goes
all in like love, the flesh
within the river's glove.

Changing of the Guard

In Brixton, from the 6th floor balcony,
early mornings you could see them
slipping home in ones and twos
along the rooftops of the nearby houses,
the urban foxes, while on the streets below
the rising populace headed off to work,
entirely oblivious to their presence.

I've often thought about it since,
that shift-work changeover,
the sleepy morning crew with their then
still-novel Walkmans at full volume,
the crackle and static you'd hear
as they passed you, running for the Tube,
while, overhead, unseen by almost all of them,
the floating brushes of our fellow residents
painted the skyline a rusty red
then vanished, in the blink of an eye,
like so many who made that country what it is.

for Katriona and Veronica

A Goat Song

When the dog begins to bark
like a thing possessed
in the stony clearing in the gorse,
knowing something must be close
I draw him back and hold him.

In moments, there they are:
first horns, then black and white,
then sand- and straw-
and wood-coloured little elfin heads
lifting above the thorny crowns
and yellow blooms
with their heady, coconut smell,

and, to my surprise,
despite the dog's alarm
and their evident nervousness,
still inching, slowly, ever closer.

Turns out, as the young shepherd
will explain (appearing,
like her charges, out of nowhere),
wild goats, when startled, make
for higher ground, and higher ground
is exactly where we've gone
and plonked ourselves,
the mutt and me.

Now, risking nothing,
with both hands firmly clamped around his lead,
all those same pictures
I've come up here to take

of sky and sea will only ever capture
sky and sea — no hint
of this unexpected presence
in the margin of the eye,
this odd encounter, the goats
like smaller, shaggy gods,
up here forever, biding their time,
standing their ground
like a council of elders
chewing over what to make
of these chinless, beardless,
hornless interlopers,
who come weighed down
with bags and baggage,
who come in bondage,
shackled one to another
like prisoners who hope to study
what it means, this being free.

A History of Pigeons

1.

Start with birds.
Most days do —
the call, the cry,
the calligraphic
blessing from the sky

before they land
or simply are:
before words, often,
before things
begin to mean —
on twigs, on branches,
arrivals, settlings,
things of nothing,
reason enough to sing.

2.

When a bird, mid-flight,
1969 or so, I'm guessing,
drops an ice cream-
textured shite
into my hair, my eye,
(I'm six, at most,
and horrified)
a neighbour jokes
that I've been blessed —
blessed, of all things —
picked out for luck,

anointed as if, who knows,
by the Holy Ghost —
God in the form of a dove
or a filthy pigeon, more like,
has brought his sloppy liquid love
to bear in my ample hair,
in the corner of my eye,
his cream and white and grey-white
spatter, his splatter,
his obscene sacrament,
his butthole's
jettisoned *lacrimae rerum,*
his, dammit, can I say it,
angel's delight.
But blessed,
they tell me I am blessed.

3.

When we were kids
in the lower yard
the pigeons cooed
and shat their small hearts out
over everything.
And when the local lads
came to carry them off,
our parents were only glad
to see them gone.

But once we humans loved them,
and the skies were blessed.
And when we wrote our notes
and codes and tied them
to their delicate, wire-thin legs

and sent them off in sunshine
or in storm into the great unknown —
gestures from our hands, our thoughts
in flight — every fluttering return
came as a miracle, every sighting
and shadow-cast and landing,
every shuffling and ruffling
of feather and wing on window ledges
and rooftop coops
updates to the book of news
we'd held our very breaths
while waiting for,

until the telegraph, the telegram,
the radio, the telephone
announced we did not need them any more,
these friends turned feral,
these scavenging servants,
these blights on town and city
now everywhere,
these filthy, shitty vermin,
these rats of the air.

4.

And then today
at St. Stephen's Green,
a man in a field of pigeons
catches my eye —
street-life wildman
or nature mystic,
difficult to decide —
but, curious as I am,
I stop to ask

(how can I pass this by?)
and when I ask
his suspicion
draws me in,
and then, without warning,
like a guest at a wedding
he leans across
to shower me
not with rice
but oats, to spill
like a blessing, an anointing,
into my hands, along my arms,
a snowfall
of oats, to smile
at and through me
as if I am not here,
as if the former me
has already left,

and I can scarcely breathe
these first few seconds,
swarmed by strangeness,
fanned by wingtip and wingbeat,
feather-swept,
and blessed, yes,
this flock of pigeons blooming
into some huge, wild and living
flowering of wings,
some smoke-and-marble
coat of many colours
two and three birds deep, birds
on my head, on my shoulders,
in the palms of my hands,
birds on both wrists, birds

in layers, in skins, in pages
and sheets, a message sent
repeatedly down the years
but until now unread,
each smallest movement,
every blink and twitch
conjuring blue-grey ecstasy
out of empty air, the wild
within reach, the shocking
flamenco fansnap
of their feathers, the delicate
pinch of sharp red claws,
the Morse code tapping of countless beaks,
the orange lights of their eyes
full on and eye-to-eye with mine
reading perch and pillar and post,
recording and erasing,
giving to and forgiving me
for all my wasted time,
for all my unfeeling crimes,
as troubles sweep the world
in waves, as Dublin
goes about its day,
as the Luas clatters by,
and the busker only feet away,
no joke, on cue,
plays 'Smoke
Gets in Your Eye' …

for Daniel Holtzochlag

Seed Bank

Svalbard Archipelago, Norway

Now, the wise ones say,
is gone. The moment you name it —
its face, its taste, its scent —
as soon as you would bless it
with a kiss, it is already
moving off, a timid creature
through the marbling light.

And so, a hundred years gone by,
to this small island in the dark
and frozen north, riding
on a woolly mammoth, revived
for onerous journeys of this kind,
I have come

to the Svalbard Global Seed Vault,
to its ice-bound metal doors to knock,
and, of the last human curators
holed up inside, to beg for mercy.
Just one single wild garlic seed
is all I ask for, to try again,
to start again from nothing …

For the legends describe
in the not-so-distant past
a path through a woodland
and a scent that would whisper *here, here now*
in the deep maze of your very being
before flare or flower might ever catch your eye.

Beyond the Hedge

Beyond the hedge at the end of our garden —
the wild lands. Donkeys and cows,
foxes and badgers, while us poor townies
made do with cats and dogs, pigeons and, now and then,
the occasional rat that ran like a blur,
like a shiver up the spine, between one old shed
and another, between a sack of new potatoes
and a stack of drying turf or wood;

like the one that someone, I can't remember who,
was said to have severed with the blade of a spade —
in my mind's eye, a budding Cú Chulainn —
the dead rat's skin-hinged corpse held aloft
like a prize on his weapon's bleeding edge,

and, afterwards, as if into the fires of hell
or the blank space at the margins of a map,
was tossed back out over our flowering hedge.

Slug

Ugliness personified,
inner tube of the wheel of life,
you ride a wave of slime, scaremongering

and gorging on the stuff of youth,
the tender leaves, the fragile shoots,
the very things that make our sore hearts sing.

Salt in the wound, we scoop you up.
We serve you beer, dumb twist in the plot,
conscript ogre of the garden's nativity play.

Feel our censure, hateful thug.
And, as your kind will, gurn and shrug.
Just be grateful that we let you slink away.

My Mother's Books

The only books that gave me pause
when my mother died were not my own —
the multiple copies in almost every room
of everything I'd written, the various editions
side by side, all that second-thinking
and inconsequential thought;

and neither the Greats
like Shakespeare (our old school plays)
or *Pride and Prejudice,* or my older brother's
long-outdated children's encyclopaedias, not even
her numerous crossword puzzle dictionaries
(as if the future were a verbal mystery
she might solve).

No, the things that made me weigh
the true value of the contents of those
last few dusty bookshelves boxed away
and ready for donating to the world
were the slim and flimsy and, it must be said,
distinctly amateur publications
from her many years as a literacy volunteer —
My First Job, My First Home, My First Car — by far
the most important books in someone's life,
and therefore, I'm proud to say, in hers.

WWF*

Like the bulked-up wrestlers my nephew
as a youngster was so obsessed with
once upon a time, here in the shade
under the lower branches of the hedge,
two armoured, carbuncled, utterly dramatic
(on whatever scale you like) common or garden lice
are now, apparently, engaged
in a fight to the death.

Thus, when I hunker down,
above their heads
on the cantilevers, the beams and trusses
that hold this whole incredible
stadium of growth in place,
the white-pink and pink-white flowers
become the floodlights, and all full on. *And …*
'Morning,' my newspaper-carrying neighbour passes by
and gives me a curious glance. 'Eh,
morning…' I reply. And wait. And wait a little longer.

… and the crowd goes wild.

   for Kirk, on his 40th

---

   * *Until a legal dispute with the World Wildlife Fund forced a change of name in 2002, World Wrestling Entertainment (WWE) was formerly known as WWF (World Wrestling Federation).*

The Concert

It starts
with a dazzling light show,
a rumbling eruption of drums,
a crescendo of strings ...
Just hours from here
the screech of rockets
through open skies,
while we sit and listen,
observing
musicians at play,
hoping for sense
from the sound,
the hypnotic precision.

And, afterwards, silence
turned up, we drive
home through the bright-lit
spic-and-span nighttown
of shades and reflections
where debutant girls
in their glittering gowns
run higgledy-piggledy
giggling through the rain.

A School

Think about that. A school. Think about
the school *you* went to. Where you sat.
Who you sat with. Your circle of friends.
The small desks for one or two.
The ink, the inkwells. The globe or map
at the top of the classroom.
The blackboard. The chalk sticks and dust.

Then imagine a bomb
going off there among you, the roof
caving in, the chalk dust
rising and swirling, hypnotically blooming,
and, for these last few
precious moments of childhood,
obscuring the worst.

Chevron

In the chevron of eleven geese
following the slow curve of shore,
veering and cornering as one,
at one point goose number four slips out
(and a goose-depth lower down), then shifts
two goose-lengths further up the line,

while goose number three and — what is it? — five?
sensing what is coming next,
separate a goose-length up
and a goose-length back, respectively, to let
their sister or their brother slip back inside —
and all the while no fuss, a few quacks,
but not a beat missed or stitch dropped.

And now at last they're back in V formation,
passing us down here below, passing
the clubhouse, passing the tower of stones
near the end of the beach (that someone rebuilds
each time it falls), passing majestically
right out over the tip of Cush Point itself
where sand and water sift and drift
to blur the line, until — and I'm squinting now —
they've entirely disappeared from view.
                              Who knew
before we walked out here this morning
to ease our heartache that this
is all it would take — no answers, no solutions,
just this simple falling into sync, this glimpse
of common purpose, this wordlessness
postponed and overdue.

for Martin Enright

Girl With a Pearl Earring

It's not about the afterlife of art,
the mystery of some bright-eyed servant girl
or the celebrated artist who chose to paint her.

Now, when it comes scrolling into view —
Girl with a Pearl Earring — it's you I see
after the latest punishing round of chemo:

tired, that brightness faded, a little older,
you brace yourself to face the world, reduced
but undaunted, that last glance back over your shoulder
at everything, against the odds, you've made it through.

Thatched Roof

In the entire town
just one thatched roof remains,
token of a past long lost,
and passing it, it feels
as if we'd just awoken here
to find ourselves transported back
to days when knowing how to lift and trim,
to bring and batch together
into sheaves the loose, undisciplined
but full of promise breeze-, wind-,
rain- and all-weather-proof cover
proffered by the fields
to those with knowledge
of where to look and when
and how to proceed
was all it took.

The one thatched roof, then,
and, beneath, I'd guess
(from the glimpsed-in-passing new extension)
a modern home, a kitchen
with all mod cons, the past
sheltering the present.

So when you walk out here,
slow down. Permit the eye
to linger for a time in praise
of things remembered, things gathered,
of golden summer evenings honoured
by a home as sacred as a church,
the honey-coloured thatch
cropped-close, lashed-down and made fast
so that those who pass by day

might be calmed, refreshed,
or, by night, last thing before they sleep,
be put in mind that, though we lie
in sheets indoors, we dream,
as do all creatures, beneath the stars.

The Mistake

One power-cut storm night
almost fifty years ago, I set
a dancing candle down beside a drape
and might have burned the whole place
to the ground.

Even now I see my parents' startled faces,
my dumb mistake itself a kind of flame
set down in the dark to light a scene
that, though half a century has passed,

remains so bright, so clear
I might yet replay that moment
their initial looks of fear
turned first to something closer to relief
then, in a flicker, turned to love again.

Late September

The gasp for air,
the grasped-at chances,
the whirr of thoughts
and blur of branches —
the heart playing catch-up
until you are caught up
and need to stop.
Then the slow walk
of revelation:
in Rush — what rush?
in Lusk, the dusk
on amber fields;
in Donabate
they've done a deal
where no one's bothered.
In Skerries
the merry sailors
sit gazing out to sea.
As for The Naul,
they're always ready
for tunes and the craic.
Enjoy it, sisters, brothers,
September's linger,
the soul's fine weather
come round again
where you're at last 'in time',
brought down to earth
not with a bang
but like a feather.

for Desmond Traynor and Jane Humphries

ACKNOWLEDGEMENTS & THANKS

With a few exceptions, the poems in this book were 'written' on my phone's Voice Memos app while out walking, exploring or observing something out-of-doors, a practice I'd already begun to employ, and enjoy, but which was reinforced during the Covid-19 lockdowns and travel restrictions of 2020 and 2021. Some poems conceived as short poetry films; of these, a number have won prizes or have been shown at poetry and film festivals in Ireland and abroad. These include, in no particular order, *Irish Film from Home, St. Patrick's Film Festival London, International Video Poetry Festival,* Athens, Greece, *Bloomsday Film Festival,* Dublin, *New York Flash Film Festival, REELPoetry,* Houston, Texas; *Verga Film Festival,* Sicily; *Kerala Short Film Festival, Shine International Film Festival* and *Gaia Film Festival,* India; *Hombres VideoPoetry Festival,* Italy; *Vaasa Wildlife Film Festival,* Finland; *IndieCork Film Festival; Vesuvius International Film Festival,* Italy; *Goa Short Film Festival; Bayelsa International Film Festival,* Nigeria; and *Inheritance – The Environmental Film Festival,* Ireland. Sincere thanks to all the programmers and organisers who took a risk with an amateur, one-person production. Sincere thanks to the programmers and organisers who took a risk with an amateur, one-person production

'The Statues of Emo Court' was commissioned as a poetry film by Michelle de Forge, Dunamaise Arts Centre in 2020. 'The Mistake' was commissioned by Bernadette Greenan at Linenhall Arts Centre, in 2021, and 'Out of the Blue' was commissioned in 2022 by Fingal Poetry Festival, with special thanks to Enda Coyle-Greene and Ernestine Woelger. 'The Statues of Emo Court' and 'Building the Ark' were subsequently issued as single-poem illustrated volumes by Orange Crate Books, with illustrations drawn from the films themselves. These, and more of the author's other films, may be viewed at *www.patboran.com.*

'Hedge School', 'Seed' and 'Back to School' were first published in *The Irish Times*. The title poem was afterwards issued as a limited edition postcard, later in audio form for Saolta Arts' online *Menu of Poems 2023* (produced by Margaret Flannery). It was also the inspiration for a beautiful piece of public art in Baldoyle by artist Stephanie McGuinness, commissioned by Baldoyle Wild Towns (special thanks to Mary Harkin, Nike Ruf and others on the team). The poem also appears in the anthology *Gratitude,* edited by Sister Stan (October 2024). 'The Window Seat' was commissioned by Laois Arts Office to celebrate the 10th anniversary of Laois Arthouse, Stradbally in December 2021, and a beautiful hardbound anthology publication, *In trust. In gratitude. In hope,* including the poem and the many artworks inspired by it, was published by the Laois Arts Office to mark the occasion. 'Seal' was published in *Strokestown Poetry Anthology 4,* edited by Margaret Hickey. 'Fellow Travellers' was a contribution to *Trauma and Identity in Contemporary Irish Culture* (Peter Lang Reimagining Ireland series, 2020, edited by Melania Terrazas Gallego, University of La Rioja, Spain). 'Driving South' appeared in *Blue Mountain Review* (ed. Clifford Brooks). 'The Scythe' and 'The High Window' appeared in *The High Window* (ed. David Cooke).

Special thanks for their continued interest and support to Laois Arts Officer Muireann Ní Chonaill, Michelle de Forge at Dunamaise Arts Centre, Madeleine Casey at Irish Film London, Paula Meehan & Theo Dorgan and others too numerous to mention.